Frangipani Frappe

KIRTIPRIYA

BLUEROSE PUBLISHERS
India | U.K.

Copyright © Kirtipriya 2024

All rights reserved by author. No part of this publication may be reproduced, stored in a retrieval system or transmitted in any form or by any means, electronic, mechanical, photocopying, recording or otherwise, without the prior permission of the author. Although every precaution has been taken to verify the accuracy of the information contained herein, the publisher assumes no responsibility for any errors or omissions. No liability is assumed for damages that may result from the use of information contained within.

BlueRose Publishers takes no responsibility for any damages, losses, or liabilities that may arise from the use or misuse of the information, products, or services provided in this publication.

For permissions requests or inquiries regarding this publication, please contact:

BLUEROSE PUBLISHERS
www.BlueRoseONE.com
info@bluerosepublishers.com
+91 8882 898 898
+4407342408967

ISBN: 978-93-5989-532-1

Cover Design: Sadhna Kumari
Typesetting: Pooja Sharma

First Edition: September 2024

Frangipani Frappe

Dedication

To Mrs. Devika Pillai, the pillar of strength that cradled my heart throughout highschool, and whose gentle assurances possibly gave me the strength to smile.

Thank you ma'am. You've put the stars in my eyes and joy in my work.

Aegroto, dum anima est, spes esse dicitur.

It is said that for a sick man, there is hope as long as there is life.
Roman statesman, s Cicero (106-43 BC)

1

Purple wool, purple crochet hook.
Gossamer hair ties. Your eyes take away my fear of swimming.
Together, we'd live a perfect lie.

2

On the little country road tucked behind the forest groves
Lived a perfect straw family.
In a white little cottage, shutters perfectly beige.
The second son could not smile,
The first one thought he couldn't do anything right.
The straw mother insisted
They were perfect.
The father told them this was the only way to live life with no regrets.
Life continued to make an effigy of them all.

3

There's butter in my soda, vinegar in my cheese.
Tears wrung out from washing cloth.
Not enough please.
There's love in my heart: we've been dancing all night.
It's been perfect, just divine.
On the way home you break me.
Bolstered by joy, I resist.
But between now and then the floor doesn't offer comfort.
Demons are all quiet now, fearful.
I can't comprehend myself from your perspective
But then again, you can't get that a smooth mouth could contain a million
Shattered screams.

4

There's coffee on my table, cold, sweet, syrupy.
There's coffee on your table.
Water so black that the universe might come out of it.
There's coffee on her table,
Plain, classic, eternal.
There's coffee on his table,
The latest in-house signature.
There's coffee on their table.
Economical little paper cups.
Another tool in midst of plans.
There's coffee on our table.
What a mix-matched dozen.
But somehow it seems more nourishing.

5

Four years I knew you.
Your laugh ignited mine.
In the dreary dark, your warmth pieced me together, across time.
Four years since I met you.
Same records for us, starting the news together
Four years since you saw me.
The puzzle pieces don't fit the same anymore.
Two years since we last spoke.
Since you made light come in.
Since the glorious gossip.
Since the weirdest wonders.
I don't know what hurts me the most
Your blank stare
Or
The mouth that
Smiles no more.

6

I'd consider you dandelion
The way you'd shatter in the wind.
I'd consider you a rock, the way you made me crack up.
I'd consider you a home, the one I trespassed through my phone.
I'd stay up, night after night.
For my favourite knight.
I have held you through the fragrant blossoms
And the terrible dragon fire.
I've liked you, admired you and loved you.
Perhaps you truly are the best.
For when I most needed a knight.
You weren't there.
Just like the rest

7

Such blue eyes.
Beautiful to behold.
Such a kind face; warmly that mouth spoke
Would the ears pick up the cries
Of your loved ones at the funeral pyre?

8

Hello? You are at my terrace.
Curled up – although
I long for your embrace.
There're stars sprinkled in your hair.
I wish to run my hand through.
Dig in your scalp
Till it turns painful
Drag you out from the stars and the night
From the shade of twilight
To the warm Sunny afternoon
Where everything was just right
Raat ki Rani; The magnificent queen of the night
Blooms gloriously
You put out the water under the moon.
And she makes it astringent
I wish I could open your throat and pour the boba cha I had laboriously prepared.
Till brown overcomes the black.
So that everything you now gained.
And all that I lost
would be reverted back.

9

People are not a filler for your time.
Let them go – let them live.
And ask why you can't bear to sit with yourself.
Do not shackle them or prison them in a cage.
If you grip them in throes of loneliness.
Ask why that in such atrocious embrace
You still can't
Show them the kindness they deserve.
When the bird flaps wings against your hands
Let it race against the winds.

10

Raven hair, mahogany skin
Emotive eyes fill to the brim.
You turn your back to salvation.

11

If patriotism runs in soil.
Why do you allow it to erode?
If nurturing children's dreams is the highest form of patriotism,
Then is breaking their spirit the highest treason?
To value breaking of bones
And to reset it in
Pre-approved moulds
What genius does the world behold?
Where my virtue comes pre-packaged
And my layers are not recyclable—can't return to the soil I came from.
I want to have steel in my nerves and bones.
You say I am depleting your ores.
Is paradise not supposed to be my home?
My blood is a betel juice red
Thickened by mud near the creek
Where bovine tread
To be ideal and elastic
The neurons need to turn into some sort of ductile micro plastic which the god beneath my ribs knits
Tick tick tick
Into some sort of world stabilizing stick

12

Rain is splashing in
thudding at the door
running down the floor
But oh darling, you are not home.
The Sun is beating in
Fading the photograph kept at the desk.
They say drought might be a coming
You do not answer your phone.
It was so windy yesterday evening
Blowing west and east
I wonder what lies beneath
Of your refusal to meet?
The snow sparkles in the meadow
The frost swirls
The icicles frame our window
The home beseeches its widow.
The stars waltz
The wind hums
The sea drums
To a strange beat
There's no name at the door, only peat
If you look further into the moss you'll find
where our buried memories weeps.

13

There's such a quilt of colourful patches.
It's supposed to be all unique.
This one throws me off
Why did you sew these textures intertwined?
This fabric next to it stained with splotches of wine
The colours together before had remained unfathomable
My life perfectly placed like pawns on the chess table.
Why did you show me a new pattern?
A new way of thinking
A new set of actions
knowing,
Now I can never use the old ones?

14

The rain is icy
Running down my warm skin
Seizing me in a hypnotic hold
It thrashes against the window.
Like a lover wanting to get in
You are deep in your head.
Voice warm and powerful
Dangerous, treacherous, vile
even makes me wish that I knew what lays ahead.
The rain is banging on the roof now
Pleading you to get away.
If you can pretend to be predator,
I can be the victim, nay?
If only you had been to the murky marshes around
The dark blue mountains towering; like soldiers standing their ground.
Against the riotous dead.
But fear not
You will befriend them tonight.
When all the things are done & said

15

My girlhood is not a graveyard.
It is not pierced by screams
(girlhood, error.)
My girl hood is an anarchist's wet dream
Full of bombs made of seeds.
(girlhood, not defined)
My girlhood does not break me.
It sweeps through my life.
Mends what's right and leaves the wrong behind.
(girlhood, page not found)
My girlhood shakes me
Shatters me
It leads to an ache in my neck
Put your plans on brake
(girlhood, limit tending to infinity.)
Contrary, my girlhood does not make me meek or defiant.
It finds and preserves
(girlhood, try searching for something else?)
The seeds of humanity
Nurtures it
To flourishment
For the orchards of trees of life to bloom.
(girlhood, godhood)

16

Flowers burst out of my armpits
My eyes and ears
My mouth and my crotch (Peeking as well through my derriere)
The vine, studded with leaves and thorns
On the skin that was too dark to adorn
Snakes and pierces through the collar bones
There's swirls of vines, fruit and blooms

Annotating down my thighs
Like whorls

The pain reminds me I'm alive
And grounds me to the earth.
Plants me deep.
There are little white flowers between my toes
Soon moss shall devour my nails
The Sun, the wind,
The Moon and the rain
push and prod
love and nurture
My existence into the immortality.

17

Such a terrible fantasy
The existence of you and me
Such a tragedy of longing
For the girl I envision to be
Hasn't snaked an arm around you
Held you tight, kissed you deep
The world rushes by
Pixels rush in my ears
While her visage is an aspiration,
Yours is steeped in satire and caricature.
Darling mine, let me weep under your gaze.
Let us kiss in the haze
I'll kiss your raised, rugged scars
And you kiss my pixelated ones.

18

Darling, the glass wall of this grocery store
is fogging from the inside.
You're out in the torrents.
Nay an extra-ordinaire, nor pulling flowers straight out of the sidewalk.
Yet I want to lose my warmth of my spring & summer.
To tread & submerge in your marshes.
Drowning in mud.
To get a glimpse of you again.

10

Why do I write myself as gentle instead of being hungry?
As if showing a dainty face with gentle smiles
will take away the eyes that ravage.
As if the bright lilt will distract the screams of anger & ambitions
Why do I have to convince myself
to be the pretty pot full of opulent flowers
to be placed at the table.
Why not simply be and have a seat?

20

I crack open the spine of this journal
Slit open my soul.
Write down the gratitude to the universe that I owe.
In hopes in prayers that if I pull it all form murky inky depths of my eyes
There'd be a flashbang
A nothingness so painful.
& the universe will alter itself to run its claw through threads of my destiny
Bewitch beloved fate again, woo her for me.

21

Through the green bramble.
Tied up in neon eyelets,
There's the desperateness of yours to connect
To reach for another soul
To breach self-imposed walls
Yell out, all is right, I'm here.
Soothe the helplessness of rebuff
Oh savior, oh beloved
Not take away the refuge
But use that hand to pull them into the land of living.
The bramble shudders
The thorns sway the youth beloved into blinding dark & dull flashes
The world's a technicolour mess
Pinpricks of muti media
Swirl by.

22

Rooted, submerged
Rooted submerged
Make a break for the surface
But oh the ocean's so cool.
Chilled iced bones
Coral & kelps
Don't pull me out – or I may break again.
Rooted submerged
Rooted submerged.
Heed the mankind's wails
(rooted submerged)

Whisper out the last breath.
Refill more turbid liquid
In my veins.
ice burning the lungs.
Rooted submerged
Rooted submerged
Let me come out as another young one again.

23

Broken, crushed shards of the brain
hopefully to be bound by caffeine
The zombie lumbers to waking dreams
a cruel mistress
not an ounce of mercy,
Faith has led to worse fates
And I can't help but wonder
Why men of past
were the monsters,
When their atrocities can't even
take a single letter of her name?

24

There's pain in paradise,
Oh lord, so help me.
Paradise is hard
Tell me, why the sins are so sweet?
Freedom is lonely, duty-bound, and a boring streak.
Send help, send love
send a free indulge of temptations card
All the hours
every single hour
the temptations snare me not by novelty, no
But the illusion of more mundane
Brilliance rotten
truly such a shame.

25

Let grief be an abrasion
Flow the pinpricks of blood on thin skin.
Let grief prolong for fourteen days.
Never just thirteen for her mother
I'll use my grief watered with love & sprinkled with lounging.
Slough away the dead skin
Start cracking at the lock.
That imprison me underneath.

26

Frangipanis are drenched.
Soaked through in gray
Littering the sail's murrow.
War doesn't stop
even when the vision's removed
But perhaps a slap of frangipani rain
Will lead to heaven's sequestered gates
Where finally I will set in disarming warmth
Belie rain & hail
The flood bags outside soak the worlds pain.
The fray of gauze
soil frayed to mesh
& I
But not as soul breakage, finally intone
Place order mine
The walls will sprout the frangipani
Petals swirling down the milk.
& one day,
Unwittingly
I'll drink my frangipani frappe.

27

The air burns
the dry acrid smoke sweetened by the rotten frangipani.
Head swirling, watching others as a dead child walking.
Trudging.
Dragging, too gone to be weeping
(tears are not believed here)
Place a cool hand on the glass enclosure
Watch into the woods
(You are not supposed to be here, little trickster. Conniving actress alleged, with mock weary eyes)

I try to puzzle your life into mine.
Soaked sweet frangipani hands
Letting the water stains give me away
(Those tears are not real. My life is not real, my existence carved from convincing cons—everyone else's but mine)

If only you could slip and carve the putrid
Vile flesh
Lipid oozing, capillaries willed from mercy
Sip a frangipani water
Sing under that white tree.
(Let its root pull you up from damp mud. Save your soul and tie it on a loved death, to glory gone.)
There's walking ghouls, soulless minds
(Including mine)

Frangipani Frappe

Of a place supposed to be sheltered
From death and birth
Let the feared destructive sand
Enfleurage the dripping bloody
bloody frangipaani

28

How to lose a friend

How does a girl's girl lose a girl?
Well,
You crack your skin a bit and show yourself.
You show your humanity –
Your tenderness – the reality of your existence.
You envelop her hand
Beseech.
Try to clarify, that all girls are not drama.
That friends of all genders are to be cherished
You try to show the worth of a flower, a shrub, a weed
To the one who only cares about wood.
Is lumber the only part of the forest?
Teaching a weed that they are truly more beneficial does not equate to your worth, little flower.
The worst thing you can do to such a girl
Is to show purpose
Ambition,
And generally, be happy
Let her in your reality and watch, heart held
For her decision
Her final take
Which of course concludes that you are fake.

www.ingramcontent.com/pod-product-compliance
Lightning Source LLC
LaVergne TN
LVHW041600070526
838199LV00046B/2069